## To our nine ducklings:
## Benjamin, Jordan, Oliver, Jaden, Annabel, Max, Philip, Lauren, and Alex

---

ISBN 0-9764092-0-8

First edition

Created, designed, and published in the United States. Printed in China.

Printing and production coordination by Integrated Communications, Gardena, California.

Published by In the Presence of Nature Books, P.O. Box 614, Allendale, New Jersey 07401

Contact the authors at: doug@goodellphotoart.com or www.inthepresenceofnature.com

# Duck Enough To Fly

### by
### Jim Wright
### Jerry Barrack
### Doug Goodell

*To Ruth, Hope all is ducky!*

*Jerry Barrack*

*J W*

In the Presence of Nature Books, Allendale, New Jersey

Once upon a secret lake
not far from New York City,
there were birds a-plenty,
and places for them to nest.

One of the brightest birds
was the father wood duck.
His feathers were so splendid
they could have been painted.

Mom was wondrous as well.
She had noble eyes and a way
of teaching tiny babies
to do very big things.

Each spring, Mom laid her eggs
in a nesting box on the lake.
The hole was just the size
for a Mom to fit inside.

After a month, the ducklings hatched
and their big day arrived. Mom peered out,
then called back to her babies:
Are you duck enough to fly?

11

Mom hopped atop the nesting box.
Just below, a fuzzy head appeared.
The duckling squinted his eyes,
to see sunshine for the first time.

Mom glided down to the lake
and called for him to follow.
But the water seemed so far below,
and he had never tried to swim or fly.

Soon, one of his sisters joined him.
She looked around and wondered:
What he was waiting for?
Was he a duck – or chicken?

17

While duckling boy watched,
unsure of what to do,
sister gave her wings a flap
and took a great leap of faith.

He glanced down at the lake again.
But he was so scared of heights
that his tiny webbed feet slipped.
What a way to greet the world.

21

That was it. He climbed to his feet
and bravely called: Geronimo!
Then he half-fell and half-flew
toward the wet and waiting water.

Mom beamed at her two new swimmers,
then called up to the rest.
She knew she had more ducklings,
and it was time they left home.

One, then another, then another,
they took their first giant baby step.
They stumbled, fumbled, tumbled.
They sighed, they cried – and they flew.

In the blink of a wood duck's eye,
they splashed down. Mom did a head count:
Nine ducklings had faced the test,
and passed with flying colors.

Mom proudly took her ducklings
for a paddle together. And
though they'd never explored
this strange new world before...

They were duck enough to try.

The End